Old TURRIFF

by

Alan Cooper

Duncan Balloch was tenant of the shop and dwelling house at Bridgend (above), and subsequently built the George Hotel (illustrated on page 7) nearby.

© Alan Cooper 2000
First published in the United Kingdom, 2000,
reprinted 2004, 2012, 2014
by Stenlake Publishing Ltd.
01290 551122
www.stenlake.co.uk

ISBN 9781840335798

FURTHER READING

The books listed below were used by the author during his research. None of them are available from Stenlake Publishing. Those interested in finding out more are advised to contact their local bookshop or reference library.

William Barclay, *The Cross of Turriff*, 1923.
J. Dempster, *Turriff O'er the Centuries*, 1982.
A. Fenton, *The Turra Coo, A Legal Episode in the Popular Culture of North-East Scotland*, 1989.
J. McIntosh, *The Life and Times of the Reverend William Stuart, Minister in Turriff's Old Kirk (1774–1795) and New Kirk (1795–1820)*, 1995.
Rev. T. McWilliam, *The Kirks of the Turriff Presbytery*, 1904.
Norman K. Wilson, *100 Years of Golf at Turriff*, 1996.
The Late Provost Hutcheon, extracted from the *Banffshire Journal* of 18 May 1909.
Banffshire Journal, 1845 onwards.
Turriff and District Advertiser, 1959 onwards.
Turriff and District Gazette, 1933.

ACKNOWLEDGEMENTS

The publishers would like to thank Allan Geddes for providing the pictures that appear on pages 1, 13, 14, 16, 18, 28, 29, 39, 40 and 48. The picture of Johnston & Paterson's Mart featured on page 30 is reproduced by courtesy of Gordon Cowie, and the picture of William Dickie's shop on the front cover by courtesy of Charles McBoyle.

The publishers regret that they cannot supply
copies of any pictures featured in this book.

Though there has been some confusion about George Frederick Findlater's place of birth, his birth certificate reveals this to have been Turriff, or more precisely Mill of Turriff, where he was born on 16 February 1872, the son of a miller, Alexander Findlater, and his wife, Mary Ann Clark. He came from a long line of Findlaters who were all millers, his grandfather at Mill of Auchinbadie, Alvah, his great-grandfather at Mill of Fisherie, King Edward, and his great-great-grandfather at Mill of Carnousie, Forglen. George spent some time with his grandparents, as the 1881 census shows that he was resident with them at that time. In the 1880s he moved with his parents to Aberdeen, where he joined the Gordon Highlanders in 1888. He served in Ireland and Ceylon before his arrival in north-west India where he won the Victoria Cross at the charge on the Dargai Heights on 20 October 1897. Reports in the British papers about a piper (i.e. Findlater) continuing to play after being shot in both ankles caused a sensation throughout the country. After receiving his VC from Queen Victoria and being discharged from the army he earned a large wage travelling around the country as a music hall entertainer.

INTRODUCTION

According to legend, a monastery was founded in Turriff by St Congan, who left Ireland in about 600 AD and settled at Lochalsh, from where he made missionary travels through the country. He became the patron saint of Turriff, and the twelfth century church was dedicated to him, as was one of the annual fairs. There was also St Congan's Howe on the east side of the town.

The earliest manuscript to mention Turriff is the *Book of Deer*, which belonged to the monks of Deer and includes a twelfth century Gaelic reference to 'Turbruad'. At that time, the whole of Buchan, including Turriff, was the property of the Celtic Mormaer (Earl) of Buchan. The earliest known mormaer was called Gartnach, and he gave a grant of land to the monastery of Deer in 1132, which was witnessed by Demongart, the 'ferleighin' (literally 'man of learning') of Turbruad. He was the member of the monastery who did the writing for it, and was also schoolmaster to the local children. Another document was witnessed by Cormac, Abbot of Turbruad.

In 1273, Alexander Comyn, 2nd Earl of Buchan (in the Norman line), erected a 'hospital' in Turriff and bestowed lands in and around Turriff on it. This was not a hospital in the modern sense of the word, but a religious house with a master and six chaplains. Travellers could stay there, 'which chusing for that evening's hospital . . . they thither marched' (from Spenser's *Faerie Queene*, quoted in the *Banffshire Journal*, 7 February 1922). The hospital was also a sanctuary for minor criminals, although the master was obliged to hand over for trial 'all manifest malefactors' (*Banffshire Journal*). If anyone living on the hospital's lands was executed for an offence, their possessions fell to the establishment.

An important function of the hospital was to pray for the soul of both the earl and the king; indeed it had been erected by the earl 'for the love of God and the health of the soul of King Alexander III and his own soul' (*Banffshire Journal*, 31 January 1922). John Comyn, 3rd Earl of Buchan, fought for Edward I against Robert I, but was defeated in a battle at North Mains of Barra, Inverurie, in 1308, after which Robert devastated the Buchan lands with fire and sword. In 1328, Robert I (the Bruce) gifted the lands of Petty,

Fyvie, to found a chaplainry in the hospital to pray for his brother, Nigel, who had been executed at Berwick in 1306 on the orders of Edward I.

From about 1500 onwards the lands of the Earldom of Buchan, and the associated Barony of King Edward, were broken up and bestowed on many different owners. The most valuable property in the parish of Turriff was the Delgaty estate, and this came to the Hay family with the marriage of Marjory Fraser, heiress of Ardendraught and Delgaty, to Alexander Hay. Eventually the Earl of Erroll, head of the Hay family, became the owner of Delgaty, and the patronage of the church of Turriff, the kirk teinds and the lands of the hospital also passed into his hands. In 1627, Thomas Mitchell, the minister of the church in Turriff, 'secularised the church lands in Turriff, with consent of the Bishop, in favour of Francis, son of the Earl of Erroll, thereby very much curtailing the stipends of his successors in office, and rendering himself obnoxious' (*Banffshire Journal*, 7 February 1922). During the engagement in 1639 between Royalists and Covenanters, known as the Trot of Turriff, Thomas Mitchell disguised himself with women's clothes and hid in his church 'and was lurkinge above the syling of the church whilst the souldiours wer discharging volleyes of shotte within the churche and peircing the syling with their bullets in severall places' (*Banffshire Journal*, 7 February 1922, quoting from Parson Gordon of Rothiemay). Three men were apparently killed during the engagement; two Covenanters and one Royalist who was accidentally killed by his own men.

In 1763, the 15th Earl of Erroll sold Delgaty Castle (now Delgatie Castle) and its estate, which included the town of Turriff, to Peter Garden for £20,000. Garden's father, also called Peter, founded Gardenstown in 1720, whilst the young Peter's brother, Francis (Lord Gardenstone), was the founder of Laurencekirk. When Peter Garden purchased Delgaty he had just returned from abroad with a fortune. He died in 1785 and his son, Francis, sold Delgaty estate to the 2nd Earl Fife (of Duff House) who bought it for £53,000 at the Royal Exchange Coffee House, Edinburgh, in 1798. Delgaty estate and the property he still owned in Turriff was sold by the 1st Duke of Fife in 1889 to the solicitors Francis George of Banff and Alexander George of Macduff.

Turriff station. The railway line from Inveramsay station, near Inverurie, to Turriff was opened on 1 September 1857, when a special train composed of thirty new carriages was laid on for the directors of the railway company and a large party of guests. 'There were many signs of rejoicing and hearty cheers of welcome all along the route . . . dinner took place in the engine shed to which was attached a marquee to accommodate the company, numbering in all four hundred and upwards' (*Aberdeen Journal*, 6 September 1857). Catering for the dinner 'was in the hands of a queen of northern hostesses – Mrs Chisholm, [of the] Fife Arms Hotel' (*Banffshire Journal*, 21 February 1922). The line was opened to general traffic on 2 September. The route from Inveramsay to Turriff was 18 miles in length with intermediate stations at Wartle, Rothienorman, Fyvie and Auchterless.

Turriff was described as 'one of the busiest stations in the Great North system [with] a large overturn in passengers, goods and live stock' (*Banffshire Journal*, 21 February 1922). The station was improved in 1884 with the opening of a waiting room and the erection of a crossing bridge. An accident in 1896 resulted in the death of the stationmaster, George Duncan. 'On Tuesday evening, Mr Duncan was at his usual post attending to the dispatch of trains. The 7.17 p.m. passenger train to Banff and Macduff had been sent off, and when the line was reported clear, Mr Duncan gave instructions to the platform porter to open the points in order that the goods train, which was standing at the north platform, might draw for the purpose of shunting back waggons on the down road and into the goods yard. Mr Duncan proceeded across the rails from the south to the north platform, and, in passing between the waggons, it is surmised he had tripped' (*Banffshire Journal*, 3 March 1896). According to a witness at the inquest, Mr Duncan had fallen while trying to pass under a waggon.

The railway station and the houses in its vicinity were outside the burgh boundary until 1934, and were known as Little Turriff. The boundary was extended following a petition from 19 householders who wished to have street lighting and were concerned that their water supply might not be guaranteed. Marr's Motor Garage & Carriage Works was founded in 1865 as the firm of Mutch and Marr. When George Mutch died in 1880, Henry Marr carried on the business himself and built it up into one of the largest carriage works in the north-east. He adapted to the advent of the motor car, after which business continued as extensively as before. Henry Marr was born in Turriff, the son of a blacksmith in Duff Street, and left school at the age of twelve to become an apprentice to his father. He then went to Aberdeen, Elgin and London, returning in 1865. Marr died in 1937, aged 91 years. His sons Julius and Harry were involved in the business with him.

Station Road (now Queen's Road), c.1910. Alexander Cran started his monumental stone works in 1899, whilst continuing to operate a similar business in Ellon. In 1904 he built a house called Granite Cottage in Station Road (the two-storey building in the distance on the right), and then moved to Turriff, selling the Ellon business in 1910, having traded there for forty years. From 1924 the Turriff works were run by his son Robert, but he died in 1928, predeceasing his father by several months. Mrs Cran sold the business to Robert Milne of Aberdeen in 1934. The Old Toll Bar House, in the right foreground, probably dated from the early 1800s when turnpike roads were being constructed. In March 1920 it was sold at auction for £150 by Charles Rennie McLeod. The purchaser was John Ivallie, ice cream manufacturer.

In 1888 Duncan Balloch, tenant of the shop and dwelling house at Bridgend, bought the premises for £800 from George Ritchie, a merchant of Schoolhill. He built and opened the George Hotel nearby in 1906. This enterprise was short-lived and soon closed down, although some information about it is recorded in a report on the death of Balloch's sister, Jeannie: 'for a number of years in the early part of the present century, she was the popular hostess of the George Hotel at Turriff Station. The George has long since ceased to be a hotel, but in its hey-day it was the resort of a faithful business clientele from Aberdeen and farther south; and each year when the salmon season was in progress on the Deveron it catered for the needs of large numbers of visitors from London who returned time and again to enjoy its hospitality. Miss Balloch was always a lively and cheery hostess, and under her management the George prospered.' (*Banffshire Journal*, 2 July 1940.)

This photograph was probably taken in 1865, just before Turriff's Old Cross was dismantled and replaced. The sheriff of the county occasionally held his court here, and it is recorded that an inquest was held at the Cross of Turriff in 1557. By the 1830s the Cross was in a ruinous state, and it was repaired in 1842 with some slight alterations. When the foundation stone for the New Cross was laid in December 1865, Sheriff Watson of Aberdeen said that 'while he had gone a good deal through the country and had seen many of its Crosses, he had certainly never seen a worse specimen than the Old Cross of Turriff' (Barclay, p6). Some of the stones from the Old Cross were incorporated into the new structure. The town hall, on the left of the picture, was built in 1845 and consisted of a school on the ground floor with the town hall above. The building was renovated in 1898 when part of it was given over to reading and recreation rooms called 'The Club'. In 1920 the hall was bought by a cinema company, though it continued to be used for meetings too, and the rooms for billiards, cards and reading were in use until 1945.

When Turriff became a burgh of barony in 1512, the townspeople had the right to erect a cross and hold a weekly market (on Sundays), as well as annual fairs on the feasts of Lammas and St Congan. Until they were transferred to the Market Hill, these markets were held on either side of the Old Cross. The New Cross was built on the site of the old one, and James Duncan was both its architect and builder. Thomas Goodwillie of Elgin executed the carving of the crossetted finials, and John Anderson of Macduff carried out the plain dressing. The ceremony of laying the foundation stone took place on 7 December 1865, and was performed by Sheriff Watson of Aberdeen. 'He hoped the building would long bear witness to the good taste of its projectors and the architecture of the age. There was a pretty considerable gathering, who cheered the learned Sheriff lustily, and after quaffing a bumper to the successful completion of the work, the proceedings terminated' (Barclay, p11).

By the time this photograph was taken the town hall had been turned into a cinema, and the words 'THE PICTURE HOUSE' can be made out above the entrance. Before the town hall was built in 1845, a house called Castle Rainy (or Rennie) had stood on its site, giving the street its name. 'It was of three storeys, with an archway passing under it, closed by a strong gate. The courtyard behind was surrounded with a lower range of houses. Entrance to the two upper storeys was obtained from the court by two stone stairs, each with two landings, one on either side of the archway. The ground floor had a vaulted roof and may have been used as stables . . . Associated with Castle Rainy is the name of a lady who has come down in local history as Lucky Rainy. It is recorded that each of her sons on leaving home received her parting advice or suggestion, called Lucky Rainy's benediction. She gave it thus – Noo laddie, tak tent, look weel after yersel! Be sure 'at ye mak seeler – honestly if ye can, but mak it.' (*Banffshire Journal*, 7 February 1922.)

The historic Erroll Lodging (right) was demolished by the town council during the 1960s because it was considered that its 'permanent preservation . . . would be restrictive to traffic' (*Turriff Advertiser*, 14 April 1961). It was originally the Earl of Erroll's town house, and for a time, in the early eighteenth century, served a private academy for boys run by William Meston. He was a classical scholar and mathematician who had been Professor of Philosophy at Marischal College, Aberdeen. A supporter of the Jacobite cause, Meston was briefly governor of Dunnottar Castle, but on the collapse of the 1715 rebellion he found refuge in Turriff in the employment of Mary, Countess of Erroll. In 1948 the 23rd Countess visited Turriff with her husband, Iain Moncreiffe. 'Mrs Shirreffs conducted them through the Erroll Lodging in High Street and part of the dungeon from which a tunnel communicated with the Old Church. At the back of the house they saw the crest of the Hay family bearing the date 1590, the date of building by Francis Hay, the then Earl of Erroll.' (*Banffshire Journal*, 5 October 1948.)

William Gammie was born in the parish of Monquhitter and served his apprenticeship as a chemist and photographer in Turriff before going to London for a short time. When he returned to Turriff he worked as a photographer for George Milne, chemist, at 45 High Street, until he opened his own shop at 15 High Street in 1892. Six years later he built a new block of buildings on the site, consisting of a shop (above, in the distance) and dwelling house (no. 13) for himself, along with new premises for the Union Bank. He was a Justice of the Peace for Aberdeenshire and, at one time, a burgh magistrate. He was also a parish church elder from 1912 and superintendent of the Sunday school. William Gammie died in 1945, aged 88. The bulk of the pictures in this book are reproduced from postcards published by him and featuring his images. George Smith started out as tenant of his shoe shop at 29 & 31 High Street (with its gable end facing the camera), but bought the premises in 1908. The purchase included the part of the property that was occupied by Mr Davidson, hairdresser.

HIGH STREET, TURRIFF.

For many years the post office was located in Castle Street, in a house that bore the date 1674. Mr Alexander was postmaster from December 1864 until his resignation in 1897, and an early letter-carrier was Eppie Massie, a sister of the town drummer, Willie Gillespie. The new post office was opened in December 1899 and was built on a site leased from Provost Hutcheon, 'the site selected being that on which the pork house stands . . . a front office for the public measuring about twenty feet square will be erected. This portion will be built upon the site of the present ice house . . . over these a dwelling-house will be provided' (*Banffshire Journal*, 8 November 1898). A. Cassie & Son, butcher, probably opened for business in the early 1930s. Alexander Cassie farmed at Backhill of Drachlaw and his son, Alex, carried on the butcher's business. Another son, Wallace, subsequently took over the farm.

John McDonald served his apprenticeship in Turriff and then went to Glasgow. Soon after returning he opened his own shop at 16 High Street (above) in about 1908, running the business until his death at the age of 55 in 1931. His son, J. G. I. McDonald, then continued to run the drapery, but transferred the business to Balmellie House in 1935 and rented out the premises at 16 High Street to Messrs Hay & Co. Ltd of Leith, grocers and confectioners. John McDonald's mother, Mrs Mary McDonald of Roseacre, Turriff, died in 1948 aged 101. According to a report in the *Banffshire Journal* at the time, her grandfather, John Scott, fought at the Battle of Trafalgar and saw Lord Nelson die. Her husband was employed on the Hatton estate and then went to Little Ardin, a farm that another of their sons, Allan, carried on after his father's death.

Balmellie Street, Turriff.

Gammie, Photo.

William George succeeded his father in the saddlery business at the corner of High Street and Main Street (far left of picture). The family's shop was built on the site once occupied by the first Episcopal chapel, built in 1738–1739. In 1743 the minister was William Cumming. When the Duke of Cumberland's troops came through Turriff in 1746, in pursuit of Prince Charles Edward Stuart's retreating army, the chapel's contents were removed and burned. Only the intervention of the parish minister, Andrew Ker, prevented the chapel itself from being burned. Cumming went into hiding for a year but then returned, visiting his congregation in their houses. 'Towards the end of 1748 he began holding services at the farm of Shand's Cross, where, in literal compliance with the penal enactment, he read service with only four persons in sight, and as many more within hearing as circumstances allowed' (*Banffshire Journal*, 14 February 1922). After 1746 the chapel was used as the parish school, and in 1790 had a roll of thirty pupils.

Balmellie Street with the Central Mart at the end of the street, and Johnston & Paterson's mart in the middle distance on the left, with a group of farmers standing outside. The original auction mart for selling farm animals (believed to have been an open-air affair on the Market Hill) was started by John Bell, Tyrie Mains, Fraserburgh. In 1884 he bought the weighing machine on Market Hill from William Fowlie, and opened the Central Mart, then called the Turriff Auction Mart, on 13 December 1888. In 1896 he sold the mart to Alexander Johnston, who had been his assistant for nine years. After two years of ownership, Johnston turned it into a public company of 6,000 shares at £1 each, all of which were taken up. Johnston then became managing director of the company. Additions were made to the mart in 1899 including an 85 foot long frontage and an arched doorway 12 feet wide. In April 1901, the mart, together with Rothienorman mart, was sold to the Central Auction Mart Co. of Aberdeen for £400 in cash plus 3,000 shares in the Aberdeen company.

The streets were dusty in summer and turned muddy in winter. High Street and Main Street were both tarred in May 1922, followed by Balmellie Street (above) and Schoolhill, with Fife Street surfaced the following year along with Balmellie Road and neighbouring streets. The numbering of houses began in an informal way in the nineteenth century and initially resulted in some confusion. According to a report in the press: 'In the regions of Balmellie Street and Chapel Street especially . . . each proprietor appears to have painted on numbers to suit himself, without regard to the sequence, and hence you find two or three separate houses in different parts of the street bearing the same number' (*Banffshire Journal*, 24 September 1878).

Main Street. The tailor James S. Esslemont built the premises at the near left corner of this picture on the site of an old house and shop that he had bought in March 1891. The first tenant to occupy the shop was John A. Dunn's Globe Boot and Shoe Shop early in 1893. Many buildings were rebuilt around this time. In 1896 the Union Inn, on the other side of the street, was demolished and the Union Hotel erected on the site by the proprietor George Murray. The frontage was made of grey Clinterty granite. In 1903, Murray bought the two shops next door, demolished them, and built two shops with dwelling houses above, with granite frontages to match the hotel. On Murray's death in 1909 the hotel was bought by George Simpson, a native of Mill of Auchintender, Ythanwells, who had emigrated to South Africa and fought in the Boer War. He was closely involved with the Turriff Pipe Band, and became its president. On his retirement in 1945 Simpson sold the hotel to Capt. Bryson of Dunfermline.

William Craick started his own business in 1889 when he acquired the butcher's at 4 Main Street. From about 1907 he also became the tenant of Bridgend Farm, and was well-known as a cattle dealer. Craick died at Clifton, Turriff, in 1919, aged 56, and the business was carried on by his son, William John Craick, who bought the property next door and built new, modern premises consisting of two shops with a dwelling-house above. One shop was rented out to Mr Robb, baker, and the other, no. 6, was retained. W. J. Craick died at Bridgend Farm in 1929 aged 40, leaving a widow and two children.

Main Street. Charles Duthie was born in St Cyrus in 1835 and served his apprenticeship with a firm in Aberdeen. In 1859 he joined his brother's business in Banff, and in 1864 they opened a branch in Turriff under the name W. & C. Duthie. On his brother's retirement, Charles took control of the business and was joined by his sons, William and Charles Jnr. (the latter was captain of the Boys Brigade). According to the *Turriff Almanac* for 1910, Charles Duthie had 'a large assortment of lamps to select from, finest paraffin and crystal oils . . . & fitted electric bells'. Charles died in 1913 when his son, William, became the senior partner in the business. Next door, John Fewtrell, chemist, opened in 1860, and the shop celebrated its centenary in 1960. John died in 1888, aged 58, and the business was then run by his widow. In 1903 her son Patrick came back from London to manage the business, but he died of typhoid fever the following year, aged 23. Mrs Fewtrell's son-in-law, James Inglis, became a partner in 1914.

Chapel Street was originally called Craigmire Lane. In 1772 an Episcopal chapel was built at what is now No. 16 (on the left of the picture, beyond the house); this replaced the earlier chapel that had been destroyed by the Duke of Cumberland's soldiers in 1746. The chapel was used until 1825 when a new one was built at the end of Schoolhill (where Clifton Cottage is today). In 1902, the old property was purchased by Mr Fraser, a brewer in Cuminestown, who demolished most of the chapel and built a house on the site, although by 1935 this was described as 'condemned and unoccupied' (*Banffshire Journal*, 26 February 1935). The same article observed that 'there is still seen the built-up arch of one of the old chapel windows'. The large building on the right of the picture and the one beyond it were originally the police station. The station was enlarged between 1904 and 1905 with the addition of a waiting room, charge room, cells and accommodation for a constable.

Alexander Mitchell was born in 1831 and brought up on a croft in the parish of Qrdiquhill. He became an apprentice with Messrs Duff & Son, bakers, Banff, and after completing his apprenticeship moved to Peterhead and went to the Greenland whale fishing, working for twelve months as a cook on one of the boats. He came to Turriff in 1854 to work for Mrs Johnston, baker, High Street, as her foreman. In 1860 Mitchell started on his own at 41 Main Street and built up a large and successful business. After his death in 1917, his wife and two sons, Henry and Frank, carried on the business and a grandson, Harry, became involved after Henry's death in 1936. The business was sold to William M. Skinner of Peterhead in 1946. 'In political wrangles or business affairs he [Alexander] never lost his equilibrium, he invariably closed the matter with the remark – weel, weel, gin we canna 'gree we canna strive' (*Banffshire Journal*, 30 January 1917).

William Carnegie, owner of this butcher's shop, also acted as a doctor/vet. According to a report in the press: 'for more than forty years Mr Carnegie had gone out and in among them, ever-ready in case of need to relieve suffering in man or animal, and had given his services and help without thought of reward' (*Banffshire Journal*, 15 July 1913). Mr Carnegie had a son, James, who became a partner in the business and was also a town councillor. However, in about 1923 the business was taken over by William Barclay, who had come to Turriff in 1911 to be a foreman butcher for William Craick before starting up on his own. Barclay died in 1946. In 1902 George Cheyne bought the business that became Cheyne's Market from James Barrie. Barrie had acquired the shop from its founder, George Ogg, in about 1886. Cheyne's Market was transformed in 1962 with a new plate-glass front, and three enlarged windows above.

Turriff grew up around the old church, and the High Street developed in a haphazard way. When Peter Garden bought the Delgaty estate, which included Turriff, in 1763, he immediately set about building a new, planned town with a central market square and streets leading to it. In the nineteenth century the ordinary markets were held on the second and fourth Wednesdays of the month (the latter included a horse sale). Sales of farm animals were held every fortnight, with the sales concluded by private bargaining. Auctions apparently started in 1879 when William Fowlie installed a weighing machine on the Market Hill. In 1898 Market Hill ceased to be used, and the horse market was transferred to a field adjoining the Central Auction Mart. The eleven acre Market Hill site was bought by Provost Hutcheon and became Hutcheon Park.

THE TURRA COO.

The introduction of the Insurance Act of 1911, which required employers to collect national insurance contributions from their employees' wages, led to protests around the country. On 31 August 1912, a protest meeting was held in Johnston & Paterson's Mart with Robert Paterson of Lendrum, secretary of the Turriff Protest Association, the main speaker. After the meeting effigies of Lloyd George and Henry Cowan, MP for East Aberdeenshire, were burned at the Cross. At further meetings a decision was made 'to stand by and defend any of their employees who should be prosecuted for not complying with the Insurance Act' (*Banffshire Journal*, 29 October 1912). Paterson was himself fined in September 1913 for failing to stamp an employee's insurance card. When he refused to pay, one of his cows was seized and an attempt was made to sell her in the Square on 9 December 1913. A crowd of some 1,500 to 2,000 people gathered, and in the commotion the cow ran off and the auctioneer brought in for the occasion had to hide in a stable until he could be rescued by the police.

The 'Turra Coo' was taken to Aberdeen and sold on 16 December 1913 by auction at premises at 8 Lower Denburn. This time the sale proceeded without incident, though the price realised, £7, didn't cover the expenses of the case which were over £11. The buyer, Alex Craig, sold the cow soon afterwards for £14 to James Davidson, a cattle dealer from Mill of Rora, Longside, who then collected donations to cover the cost so that he could return her to Robert Paterson. The presentation of the Turra Coo (above) took place on 20 January 1914, in a field above the Square, in a carnival atmosphere following a procession through the town, with fireworks and a brass band playing. Archibald Campbell, Mains of Auchmunziel, New Deer, made the presentation speech and Robert Paterson replied, accepting the cow.

The two red sandstone houses on the left of this picture of Duff Street were both demolished during the 1960s. The *Turriff Advertiser* for 14 April 1961 listed Nos. 19, 21, 23 and 25 Duff Street as all being scheduled for demolition. Many properties have been demolished by the town council over the years, some of them in order to widen roads and improve the flow of traffic through the town. The red sandstone buildings are a notable feature of Turriff, the stone having come from quarries near Delgaty Castle and at Ardin. The last of these was closed in 1950 after about 200 years of quarrying there. Rev. James Cruikshank, minister of the parish church, writing for the *Statistical Account* of 1843, observed that 'In Conn's quarry fifteen men on an average are employed, and the tacksmen drive a considerable trade. Quárriers earn 12 shillings to 14 shillings per week and dressers £1'.

Fife Street, Turriff.   Gammie Photo.

Fife Street with Pirie's Lane leading off to the left. At 32 Fife Street there is a sign for Clark, merchant. In 1896 Nos. 32 & 36, comprising a shop and two dwelling-houses, with a large garden, were sold at an auction in the Commercial Hotel for £356 to Mrs Stewart, stoneware merchant of Chapel Street. On the left is the delivery cart of Ritchie, baker, Schoolhill. George Ritchie was born at Mill of Melrose in the parish of Gamrie, and after serving an apprenticeship with a grocer in Macduff he opened his own shop in Turriff in 1867, to which he added a bakery business in 1894. A tenant to begin with, he subsequently bought his shop and also Balmellie House, 'the whole forming one of the most compact and valuable business properties in the burgh' (*Banffshire Journal*, 13 October 1896). Ritchie died in 1896 and the business was carried on by one of his sons. Another son, William, went to Winnipeg and was in business there. Whilst travelling home in 1915 for a holiday he was lost when the liner *Lusitania* was torpedoed by a German U-boat.

Looking down Fife Street towards the Square. The small building on the right was the White Horse Inn (its sign can be seen above the door). George Center was the licensee for 42 years until his death in 1925 at the age of 80. In 1930 the inn was bought by G. A. Hay, carpenter, Fife Street, and may have been closed at this time. Chalmers School (now a residential property at the corner of Banff Road and Chalmers Lane) was situated just beyond the inn. George, James and Alexander Chalmers were three bachelor brothers who owned a merchant's business in the town and also the estates of Dorlaithers and Greens. When the last of them, George, died in 1852, the Chalmers Trust that they had set up came into being. Chalmers School was built soon afterwards and leased from the trust until 1889 when it was handed over to the School Board. When the new school was extended in 1898 the children were transferred there and Chalmers School was closed down and sold. Soon afterwards it became the drill hall for the Volunteers (Territorials) and was used by them until 1938 when they moved to a new hall at the end of Balmellie Street.

Church Street. Work on the new parish church began in 1794 and it opened in May 1795. The driving force behind the project was the minister, Rev. William Stuart, who had been the minister in the old church since 1774 and had seen his church decay during that period. Reports from carpenters and masons were given to a meeting of the heritors in September 1792 and indicated major defects – the walls were leaning outwards and cracking in places, while the timber in the roof was rotting. Since 1794 there have been many alterations and additions to the church; a new roof was required as early as 1805, an aisle to accommodate 300 was added in 1830, a vestry was built in 1864 and in 1875 the original double belfry was replaced by a single one. At a meeting of the Kirk Session on 9 December 1929 it was decided to adopt the name Parish Church of St Ninian, and the former UF church became the Parish Church of St Andrew. Mr and Mrs James Kelman moved into the house in the foreground around the end of the First World War (their daughters Margaret and Isabella appear in the picture on page 40). A large yard and joiners workshop once stood behind the house.

It was reported in the press in 1882 that 'Manse Terrace on which three feus have been vacant for some time is to be completed this season. The feus are taken by Mr Thomson, Post Office, Mr Hans Smith, merchant, and Mr A. McKenzie, jeweller' (*Banffshire Journal*, 15 April 1882). The street was widened in 1894 when a concrete pavement was provided. At that time houses were often sold by public auction, and 6 Manse Terrace was bought for £700 in 1923 by William Stephen from the estate of the late James Thomson. No. 4 Manse Terrace was sold in 1945, in the Commercial Hotel, to Miss Cameron, Kirkton, Forglen, for £1,270. The council acquired the ground on the other side of the street and built six houses in three blocks at a cost of £5,318 in 1920.

Alexander Johnston was born in Orkney, while Robert Paterson was a native of Turriff. Both men already had experience of the auction business in Turriff (Paterson had been a cashier and clerk for seven years) when they bought the Shire Mart near the railway station in 1902. They closed this down and transferred the buildings and fittings to Balmellie Street, opening their new mart (shown here) on 16 December 1902 with a Christmas sale of pigs and poultry. Robert Paterson became involved in many businesses including saw-milling and quarrying (he reopened the Ardin Quarry at Delgaty in 1919), although he is best remembered as the main personality in the Turra Coo episode.

Masonic Lodge St Congan No. 922 was founded in 1902 with 59 members. Rev. Gunson wrote: 'When I became the minister of the charming parish of Turriff in 1901, I found the pretty, clean, town far in advance of most Scottish towns, with its public hall, church halls, club, bowling green, and golf course. One thing surprised me. There was no Masonic Order. The matter was soon put to right. An enthusiastic band of brethren founded a lodge.' (*Banffshire Journal*, 3 August 1920). Initially, the masons used a small room in the parish church hall, but as membership increased they decided to build their own temple (above). Designed by Bro. Joseph Rae, it was built of grey Pitsligo granite, and was opened in October 1925, by which time membership had increased to 300. In 1887 the horse pulling the Turriff to Aberchirder coach was frightened by an approaching traction engine in Gladstone Terrace (above) and ran the coach up against a stone wall, overturning it. The passengers were severely shaken, and one man decided to return home to Aberdeen by rail.

TURRIFF PARISH CHURCH JUNIOR GUILD.

Photo by Milne

At a meeting of St Ninian's Church Women's Guild in 1931, Rev. P. C. MacQuoid referred to the death of Jane Gammie, wife of William Gammie, the photographer and bookseller: 'Mrs Gammie was one of the oldest members of the Women's Guild. That Guild formed in 1891 during the ministry of the late Dr A. M. McLean, has played a most prominent part in the life of this church. In this place where societies and organisations rise as rapidly as Jonah's gourd and as rapidly vanish, surely the continuance of this Guild is not a little remarkable' (*Banffshire Journal*, 27 January 1931). As well as the Women's Guild, a Young Men's Guild had been formed in September 1889 at a meeting called by Rev. McLean. This organisation had been started on a national basis eight years earlier, and by October 1888 had 502 branches and 16,835 members. Members of Turriff Junior Guild are featured in this picture.

Turriff

Turriff's third Episcopal church was built in 1825 at the end of Schoolhill, but in 1862 was dismantled and the materials used to build a new church, St Congan's (above), which was opened in 1863. The chancel in the new church was built as a memorial to Alexander Jolly, Bishop of Moray, who had been the minister in Turriff from 1777 until 1788. Jolly was apparently a saintly man. Rev. James Christie, who was the minister for 51 years from 1837, told the story of how he once 'was accosted on his way by a poor man for alms. He had no money in his pocket, but observing that the beggar had no shirt on, he, in the benevolence of his heart, stripped off his linder (flannel shirt) and handed it to him' (*Banffshire Journal*, 11 January 1881). While in Turriff, Jolly lived with his sister and a brother, James, who had a shop in the town. James was drowned while bathing in the river at Turriff in 1781, aged 22 years.

Deveron Bridge and toll-house were built in 1826, and the parapet of the bridge was raised by one foot in 1908. Turriff Angling Association was formed in 1920. 'Now that the fishing season is with us, Turriff anglers are enjoying this pastime on the Deveron, owing to the kindness of Sir George W. Abercromby, who has generously let part of the water on his estate for this purpose. A new Association has just been formed under the name of the Turriff Angling Association' (*Banffshire Journal*, 20 April 1920). 'The members of the Association held a contest on Monday when quite a large number of members gathered on the Deveron . . . The first prize, worth a guinea, went to Mr Alexander Rae, postman, who had a basket of 14 trout weighing 4lb. 2oz. The heaviest fish taken scaled 1lb. 6oz. Eighteen members took part in the contest' (*Banffshire Journal*, 23 May 1922).

The Golf Club was founded in October 1895 at a meeting in the town hall, when officials were appointed and subscriptions set for the year at 5/- for men, and 2/6 for ladies. The first course which extended to 11 acres was opened soon afterwards on the Market Hill (due to the success of the new auction mart the site was no longer needed for markets). From 1899 the area was known as Hutcheon Park. Other sports also used the park, leading to some congestion. At the AGM in 1900 'it was recommended that no golf be played on the course after 2 p.m. on Saturdays as it interfered with football matches and practice (*Banffshire Journal*, 9 October 1900). In 1904 the club had 61 members, an increase of 35 on the previous year. 'On Tuesday, Mr Donaldson, the well-known Aberdeen golfer, paid a visit to the Turriff course, and engaged in a game with two local players . . . Mr Donaldson established a record for the course, completing the rounds in 34 and 32' (*Banffshire Journal*, 26 July 1904). In 1909 the course was extended, with the nine holes in Hutcheon Park being reduced to seven. The new golf course at Rosehall (above) was opened in August 1925.

GOLF COURSE, TURRIFF.

Harvesting at Skene Croft, near Turriff. The *Banffshire Journal* of 15 September 1891 mentions that 'an interesting trial of a Massey binder . . . took place at the farm of Little Colp, occupied by Mr Tarves. The machine was drawn by two horses, and taking into consideration the twisted state of the crop, the work done was satisfactory. At the adjoining farm of Lower Smiddyseat, Mr Geddes had a Bissett binder, which he recently purchased, at work. Three horses were used in this machine, and the work done was admirable. Ten acres were cut on Monday at the rate of one acre per hour. There are now some twelve binders at work in the Turriff district.' The appearance of a tractor-driven reaper was mentioned in the same paper on 17 September 1918: 'The interesting sight was seen the other day of part of the grain crop in the Turriff Haughs being cut by means of a tractor and binder. These outfits are now getting quite common, but this is the first occasion when one could be seen harvesting a crop in the near vicinity of the town. The tractor was a Fordson which, although of small size, showed ample power, and its speed and the ease with which it turned at the corners was greatly admired by the onlookers.'

The first Free Church service in Turriff was held on the evening of 11 June 1843 in the Congregational Chapel. On 26 April the following year, the foundation stone of the Free Church was laid. Following problems with dry rot in 1872–1874, and the need to carry out further repairs in the 1890s, it was decided to build a new church (above), and this opened on 22 June 1900. During the First World War the church hall was used as a VAD (Volunteer Aid Detachment) Hospital, with twenty beds, run by the local branch of the Red Cross. It opened on 30 January 1915 and after receiving some Belgian soldiers took in batches of British troops, sometimes as many as fourteen at a time. A musical recital and dance was held in the town hall on 15 April 1919 to mark the winding up of the VAD Hospital.

Turriff District Hospital was built between 1895 and 1896 and cost just under £1,400. It only catered for patients with infectious diseases, and had isolation departments at each end of the building – one for men and one for women – with an administration block in the centre. At a meeting in February 1899, it was recorded that nine patients had been admitted in the previous six months, eight with scarlet fever and one with typhoid. Initially oil lamps were used to light the hospital, but gas was installed in 1923 at a cost of £62. The hospital closed in June 1931, with the District Nurse allowed to reside there rent-free in return for keeping the wards clean and aired. The building reopened as a cottage hospital in November 1935.

In December 1886 a meeting was held in the town hall with a view to forming a Curling, Bowling and Lawn Tennis Club. Officials were appointed, and a lease of thirty years was obtained on the site of the old brickworks, which was rented from Lord Fife for the nominal sum of five shillings per year. The premises were ready by August 1887 but 'on account of the extremely dry Summer . . . it has been resolved to defer using the bowling green for a little until the turf has taken thorough hold' (*Banffshire Journal*, 23 August 1887). In 1889 a pavilion was built, along with a cistern for water and a press for holding curling stones. Later on the curling pond was turned into another tennis court (although a new pond was mentioned in 1899). The Curling Club seems to have separated from the Bowling Club about 1903, and a new bowling green was opened in May 1905.

Tennis in Turriff began in 1887 as part of the Curling, Bowling and Lawn Tennis Club. In September of that year the local press reported that 'members have now been playing on the bowling and lawn tennis greens for some weeks' (*Banffshire Journal*, 13 September 1887). After the bowling and curling had divided into two parties, curling seems to have been abandoned, while the tennis players formed their own club in 1905. A meeting was held in the town hall, with Captain Orme, Boggieshalloch, presiding. 'He was of the opinion that the green could be got from the Bowling Club on favourable terms' (*Banffshire Journal*, 9 May 1905). At another meeting soon afterwards 'it was intimated that the Bowling Club had put the tennis green in order for playing, and would grant the use of the same free, besides giving the privilege of using the pavilion' (*Banffshire Journal*, 16 May). From left to right the tennis players in this photogragh are: Alex Anderson, the late Margaret Kelman (subsequently Mrs James Robertson), her sister Isabella Kelman, and the late George Geddes. Isabella and George were subsequently married.

Opened in May 1923, the recreation grounds consisted of two tennis courts, a putting green and a quoiting pitch. The land was donated by Provost John Stewart, and the scheme cost £600. Quoits was a popular game at the time and matches were arranged against other local clubs such as Fyvie and Monquhitter – where the minister, Rev. John Ewen, started a club in 1920 and also played in the team himself. The world champion, a Mr Watters from Lochgelly, visited Turriff in May 1924. John Stewart was the owner of the bakery and grocery store at 35 High Street. He died in March 1925 and was succeeded by his son, John G. Stewart, who enlarged the business by buying the adjoining fish & chip shop belonging to Mrs Watt.

TURRIFF MUNICIPAL RECREATION GROUNDS.

GAMMIE PHOTO

When Turriff School opened in 1878 it was only a single-storey building. A new wing was added in 1892, and in 1899 it reopened as the two-storey building above. 'In 1897 steps were taken for the provision of higher education. The expert chosen to advise was Mr Walker, Chief Inspector for the District. Mr Walker reported in favour of amalgamating the burgh schools by adding a storey to the public school. . . . On the completion of the new building, the scholars were transferred from the Chalmers School, and that property was sold, Miss Brander, who had been headmistress of the school from a time prior to 1873, retiring on a well-earned pension' (*Banffshire Journal*, 21 February 1922). Chalmers School became the Drill Hall for the Volunteers (now known as Territorials) and still exists today at the corner of Banff Road and Chalmers Lane.

In 1790 Turriff parish school met in the old Episcopal chapel and had only thirty pupils; the subjects taught were English, Latin and arithmetic. 'In 1843 there were in the parish, in addition to the parochial school, three other schools taught by male teachers – one in the burgh, the others at Fintry and Lescraigie. There was also a female school, and several dame schools. The headmaster of the parochial school was the Rev. John Clark, a licentiate of the Church of Scotland. There were a hundred scholars in average attendance' (*Banffshire Journal*, 21 February 1922). The Technical School (above) cost £3,000 and was opened in 1908. Westwood House, a boarding school for young ladies, also stood in the vicinity but closed down *c*.1900. An earlier boarding school in the town was started by William Meston in Erroll Lodging (see page 10) and flourished for a time until it closed following a duel between two of its students, Mr Gordon of Embo and John Grant of Dentergas, afterwards a Major General in the Prussian army. William Meston died in 1745.

On the passing of the Education Act of 1873, George Hendry was appointed compulsory officer by the Turriff School Board. Playing truant was very common at that time and it was Hendry's task to search for missing boys. 'He generally made a point of trying the Market Hill first, giving a look into the killin' hoose in the passing, as a boy . . . was often used for doing odd jobs . . . On market days [Hendry] would observe wee Jocky Peterson earning a few coppers haudin' a stirkie while its owner went into some of the drinking booths which stood on the hill at that time . . . Whenever the zealous compulsory officer saw his victim he would circle round the back of the booths, stalking his quarry so to speak, until he could dart out on him from behind. Then all at once poor Jocky would find himself gripped very firmly by the ear, and, in this embarrassing manner was he marched down the centre of Main Street to the school where John Tamson's strap was awaiting his already tingling palm (*Turriff and District Gazette*, 3 February 1933).

John Williamson, known as 'Cockie', was the town crier and bill-poster for thirty years until his death in 1892 at the age of 50. Williamson was born at Cockmoss, a croft that was afterwards amalgamated with Woodside of Delgaty. Though an imbecile from birth, he was proud of his job and made sure that the householders were wakened early in the morning whether they wished to be or not. On the morning of the annual holiday, in August, one irate householder responded: 'Cockie, ye vratch 't ye are, fat are ye dee'in here at this time o' the mornin' waukenin' fouk oot o' their sleep wi' yer infernal bell?' To which he replied 'Train winna wyte on you d'ye think; 'way you go' (*Turriff and District Gazette*, 3 March 1933). Cockie attached himself to the local Volunteers and even wore a discarded uniform and attended the annual camps until an adjutant encountered him in Union Street, and the uniform was withdrawn. He was buried in the old churchyard, and a memorial was erected in 1892 with the epithet 'Ye winna forget me fan I'm awa' '.

The first Boys' Brigade company in Turriff was attached to the parish church and seems to have been formed soon after the opening of the church hall in November 1894. An article in the local press gives an insight into the company's early years: 'At a special parade last week in the parish church hall, the boys presented Captain Joseph Rae with a beautiful gold albert and medallion, in recognition of the great attention which he has devoted to their training for the past six years. Bandmaster Simon was also presented with a handsome medal' (*Banffshire Journal*, 14 August 1900). Another company of thirty boys, attached to the United Free Church, was formed in 1904. When Rev. Duncan Maclaren came to Turriff in 1908 only the UF company was still in existence, and under his guidance the brigade became non-denominational. The boys handled rifles until 1925 when parents nationally voted against their use. This picture has the date 11 November 1929 on the back. Officers in 1929 were Captain P. R. Mackenzie, Lieut. J. G. Macdonald and Staff-Sergt. Fraser.

TURRIFF SHOW

In the nineteenth century the haughs was a wet and marshy area used by the townspeople for grazing their cows; it was then 'a goodly sight to see fifty to sixty of the feuars cows daddling to and from the haughs' (*Banffshire Journal*, 25 October 1921). In 1882 the paper mentioned 'the congregating of cattle by the blowing of a horn, to proceed to the haughs for grass'. A Haughs Committee was formed in 1872, leasing 50 acres of land from the 5th Earl Fife with the specific intention of draining the area and bringing it into cultivation. In 1894 the committee bought the land for £1,600 from its new owners, Messrs George, and in 1921 it was handed over to the council by George Hutcheon of Gask (son of Provost Hutcheon), chairman of the committee, which was then dissolved. The first Turriff Show was held on the Market Hill on 26 July 1864 and the event was moved to the haughs in 1924.

The path along the Den was laid in 1898 on the instructions of the owners, A. & F. George, who wished to provide a public pleasure ground for Turriff. They provided seats along the path and trees were planted on the braes. In 1909 Brodie's Braes and the Den were handed over to the town council by Alexander George of Viewmount, Macduff, and Mrs George, widow of Francis George, of Ashlea, Banff. The pavilion in the picture was provided by Robert Paterson of Lendrum in 1920 and was built for dancing, which was held twice a week. Soon after being built, the pavilion was handed over to the town council. Another gift to the town from Robert Paterson was a footbridge over the Deveron, provided by him in August 1925, and giving access to the new golf course at Rosehall.

The boat of Ashogle on the Deveron, Turriff. Ashogle is mentioned in the land given by Alexander Comyn to support the hospital he founded in 1273, which was described as being: 'bounded on the west by Douern as far as the stream called Knockieburn, between Auchinsoigle (Ashogle) and Knocky' (*Banffshire Journal*, 31 January 1922). This small ferry boat provided a means of crossing the Deveron at Forglen. The postcard was sent by George and Annie Barrie and says 'This will show you my home and a new arrangement for driving the boat'.